the Art of

GIFT GIVING™

the Art of
GIFT GIVING™

written by Shereen Elise Noon
cover design and layout by Jodi Anthony

Lulu Publishing
www.lulu.com

✦✦ 3 ✦✦

Cover Design and Layout: Jodi Anthony
www.jodianthony.com

Written by Shereen Elise Noon
© 2006 by Shereen Elise Noon
All Rights Reserved.

First Edition November 2006

Published by Lulu Publishing
in the United States of America
www.lulu.com

(310) 497-0597
www.grahamstreetinc.com

ISBN 978-1-4303-0417-3

Acknowledgements

I would like to thank Aaron Star
for giving me the gift of the
Freedom & Space to Create,
Unconditional Acceptance & Forgiveness,
and a Love & Passion
Beyond my Wildest Dreams!

I am so very grateful for the Goddess, the Earth, Mommy,
Babaji, Rita, Nana, Max, Laksmi, Soreya, Kam, Jamie,
Jannie, Jehan, Zoe, Peter, Jodi, Mere, Jean, Becca, Pat,
Natascha, Charly, Pasha, Patrick, Tony, Maija, Elizabeth,
Helena, Fiona, Shelley, Heather & Scott, Susan, Zoli, Sallie
Ann, Beth & Tim, & Jesse Lynn for all their
Love, Wisdom, Laughter and Light.

Prologue

We are living in a new world – one filled with spirituality and oneness. We have more compassion and understanding for each other than at any other time in history.

We increasingly express our desire to acknowledge, appreciate, and love one another through giving gifts.

My intention in writing this book is to share new ideas, tools, and resources, which may help you become a true master at gift giving. May you be blessed a thousand fold by everything you give and everything you graciously receive.

All good things,
Shereen

Contents

the Art of
Listening

Mastering Gift Giving is All About Listening

"Listening?" you ask.

Yes, it's about listening, really listening to what people aren't so much saying, but what they're *trying* to say. Many people go on and on about absolutely nothing – and for hours.

But if you know what you're listening for, you will have the ability to uniquely touch people's hearts.

How to Listen

To listen, you must be present. By present, I mean mentally and emotionally present, moment to moment in the room, not thinking about yourself and what you did, should do, or what you're going to do or say next. Not thinking about what you did right, what you did wrong, what you said, how you showed them, or how you could have done it better. To truly hear, you must want to be present with the other person. Completely and 100% focused on his face, eyes, mouth and the meaning behind his words. It's not easy, but the rewards are priceless.

What to Listen For

Sometimes, the sounds coming out of his mouth will sound like nonsensical, mishmashed, garbled garbage. And that's okay. Just stay with him. You are on raging waters, tossed across large boulders, dodging spinning whirlpools that could suck you down forever. Just come back to the room and remember that he really is saying valuable things to you at this moment in time. Perhaps he is trying to tell you about himself and wants you to know him intimately, but safely. It could be that he has camouflaged his true self with gobbledygook and whirligigs, in order to protect himself from your possible judgment or criticism. It's an expertly smoke-screened mystery that is your exciting mission to solve.

Listening is *my* greatest challenge. I usually listen until I can figure out where he is going with this line of conversation, and then, something happens in my mind that makes me think I know everything he is going to say next. That's when I check out. My thoughts take off a million miles a minute with; something that reminds me of something else, how that affects me, what that really means about him, how I can fix him, or what was going on for me that day.

After a while, I realize his lips are still moving, but I can't hear anything and realize that I have no idea what he has been saying for the last five minutes! I try to mentally recall his last few words or even a whole sentence to see if I can fake being present the whole time. He can tell I'm not with him, but either no one really expects you to truly "get" them, or we have all become masters of half-listening and half-expecting to be heard. We usually just go on as if I didn't just miss a huge chunk of the conversation.

Listening takes lots of practice, but luckily we've all got nothing but time filled with people talking to us! Every conversation is an opportunity to stretch the "being present" muscles. With every attempt, you will get better. Soon you'll hear whole conversations without missing a nuance. The richness of this kind of connectedness and intimacy is extremely rewarding, for you and the person you care about. It can nourish the soul like nothing else.

For now, however, you're on a quest: to find wonderful ideas for gifts to give him. Listen to his heart, not his mouth. The answers are there if you really want to master this art. Only here will you find, out of the myriad of material objects that exist in this world, the answers to what gift might make him happy. This is not a practice for the self-obsessed or shallow of heart. This is a mission for the most courageous and daring warriors. For those of you who are brave enough to see and accept another person exactly as he is, you may find that this skill could be your greatest gift to humanity.

TURNING OFF THE PROJECTOR

Most of us have no clue how to truly see who's right in front of us. We're usually looking through a thick fog of our own projections of our inner narratives, stories, over-analysis, confusion, and worries attempting to win the day for ourselves. We see others through filters fogged by our mistakes, goals, frustrations, dreams, angers, desires, and hopelessness. We feel, "I can't accept what I don't like about myself or my life, so I'll project it out into the world onto other people, and attack it on that battlefield."

By escaping and denying our own issues, we never get to master the art of seeing other people clearly, let alone ourselves. We're only half here. We have so much fear about being emotionally harmed directly or indirectly, that we can barely look one another in the eyes. If we do, it's only for brief moments, and then we look away for relief and safety. But we can get through the fog by being present for as many moments as possible each day, setting aside our concerns long enough to see who the amazing person is right in front of us.

Imagine this: take your projections of your mental worries, voices, thoughts, criticisms, and judgments, and run them through a powerful filter that screens them completely out of your vision. Imagine that that filter is completely coated with all of those thoughts. Now remove the filter and set it carefully into a strong, lightweight steel box, bolt it with three big locks, and place it in a room behind a heavy wooden door where it will be safely stored. Know that all your thoughts about what you need to fix, solve, or be right about, are secure and contained, available for you at a later time. You can come back to them and put the filter back onto your projector right after you're through being present with this person. But for now, you're unencumbered, feeling free, light, and clear.

Ahhh, that's better.

Close the door behind you and see everything exactly as it is. Things may seem a little quiet to you. The voices have stopped. You're here now. You can be present and focused on these valuable moments with your friend. Make physical contact, look him in the eyes, and let him into your heart.

See him as if for the first time. Hear him as if for the first time. Love him as if your heart is stretching wider than the universe. Feel how great you are. Remember how much you have to give and how much you want to give.

GETTING BUSTED AND TURNING OFF THE PROJECTOR, AGAIN!

Sometimes I'm so consumed with my day, my issues, and my plans on how to keep the world spinning on its axis that my filter will bust out of the box, break down the door and fly right back onto my projector right in the middle of a heartfelt conversation! And I won't have any connection to where I was, when I was, or what happened for maybe the past five minutes. I can tell when my boyfriend catches me. He gets an annoyed look on his face, and I start coming back, realizing I've been busted. And then I back peddle. Of course, it doesn't work, so let me tell you up front, it's just a lot easier to "out" yourself.

I tell him, "I'm so sorry, I wasn't being present. I got lost in my head. I care about what you were telling me. Would you please say it again? I will really listen this time." He'll be a little irritated with me still, but it goes away quickly, because he knows that I'm being sincere.

Something like that, in your own words ends up getting you back to the starting point a lot faster than trying to fake it. Plus, you lose a lot of trust points, if you're not honest and direct. Okay, get that filter locked up in its box and get present!

the Art of Caring

WHAT DOES THIS PERSON MEAN TO YOU?

Now that you know what matters to this person, it's time to ask some questions of yourself. Who is this person to you? Why does she matter to you? Do you really care if you get her the perfect gift or not?

It's alright if you don't care. Most of us are too busy to shop for more than dearest friends and immediate family. Maybe this person would be perfectly satisfied receiving an Amazon gift certificate from you, believing that you really understand their love of books or music.

But, if you find some really good reasons why she matters to you, for example; you love her and care about her life and her welfare, you'll want her to be happy and be in your life for a long time. Maybe you care more than you realize.

EXCITED EMOTIONS ARE YOUR BIG CLUE!

You are learning a new language, but you will receive BIG CLUES. As you ask this person questions such as how her day went and what interests her, and as you listen intently to her answers, pay attention to the little things. Your friend may be getting excited. The more you listen, the more she seems to be wandering deeper and deeper into her thoughts, feeling safer, because you're creating a space for her to feel heard and worthy of your attention. You have no idea how rare this feeling might be for her. You may be the first person in years or even decades who truly listened and heard what she wanted to share. And as she takes you down her private road, your friend is feeling *emotional excitement*.

Because you are still being 100% present with her, she may speak faster, more intensely, and with greater emotion. This is your BIG CLUE! You are getting close to what really matters to her. Now really pay attention, because in this excitement you can see glimpses of what she wishes someone knew about her – anyone, especially you. This is your chance to read between the lines – to really get her.

And this is when your ego will strongly urge you to "check out." But you won't, because you're mining for gold. And it's right here, right now – right in front of you, if only you will stay present.

Whatever glimpses you get, mirror them back to her. You could respond with, "It sounds like you really had a hard time believing you could make it through that river." And then watch what happens! Either, she will say, "NO! You're not getting this," or she'll say, "Yes, and it was so great to overcome blah, blah, blah and I didn't know that I could blah, blah, blah…"

If she gets frustrated with your missed translations, don't take it personally. You're in new territory and being patient and persistent will get you to your destination. Let her know your intention is to understand her accurately, that you value what she is thinking, and behave as if you have all the time in the world to get it right. This will calm her down and grow a new kind of trust in you when she realizes that you respect her enough to set aside your stuff and listen to what matters to *her*.

She is giving you her precious treasures as she lets you see into her most vulnerable ideas, feelings, and inspirations.

Now you have something. You have an idea of what has meaning in her life and how she sees things. The more you listen, the more options you have to find the gift that will make her wrap her arms around you and weep. This is the ultimate reward of being a Master Gift Giver.

Keep a
BIG CLUE List
Close By

You may want to make a list of all the people in your life who really matter to you and what matters to them, and keep that list close. You could add little notes next to their names every time you get a BIG CLUE about what they may enjoy. Or add new names whenever you remember someone else you care about. Keeping everything in one place is a great way to create an effortless system that works. Then when you need it, you know exactly where to look.

Do whatever makes your life simpler.

I like writing my list of BIG CLUES on the back of business cards, because they fit into my wallet easily and I know where to find them to quickly jot down more ideas. And I always have my purse and wallet close by.

If you're on your computer, and you find the perfect gift for someone on the web, create a new folder called "Big Clues" under "Favorites" at the top of your web browser. It keeps things confidential, too!

There are so many things we think we're going to get to someday. Let's start a list right away. We only have today and there are no guarantees. It's within your power to let everyone you love know it, and as often as possible. Honor them now by taking the time to create an easy way to keep track of who *they* are and what *they* love.

NANA

When I was eight years old, we were all sitting around the Formica kitchen table at my grandparents' home in Michigan eating lunch. I looked at Nana standing by the fridge and I realized that she would not always be around. I jumped up, squeezed her as tightly as I could, and told her how much I loved her. She was so surprised and delighted by my spontaneous expression of love. I could see how happy it made her.

When I was 13, Nana died of lung cancer, and even though it was so terrible to lose her physical presence, I've always known deep in my heart that she knew how much I loved her. I've never had one drop of regret that I missed an opportunity to show her how much she meant to me. Even now, I feel her close.

There's a feeling of completion and wholeness that comes from saying or doing the things you want to as they come up, instead of procrastinating until that "better" moment. There just is no such thing.

This is it. Right here, right now.

WHY DOES IT MATTER TO THEM?

Do you know how your loved ones feel? Have you ever put yourself in their shoes? It's called *compassion*, but it's more about what you would feel like if you were in their exact circumstances, had their past, lived the way they did, experienced life through their eyes. What makes them happy, sad, lonely, or inspired? What do they yearn for and what do they dream of when they dare to dream? What is their highest vision of themselves when they're all alone? What do they sing about when they're in the shower? What is their biggest regret in life? What are they afraid they won't have the chance to do before they die?

the Art of Creative Thinking

Now that you know what's most important to this person, you've received your BIG CLUES.

On a normal day, you are extremely busy and remembering these moments are probably not your priority, so as soon as you have a chance, write it all down! Anywhere actually, just so it's in writing. You may remember these things later, but in case you're enjoying the present moment so much that you forget the details, it's helpful if what really matters to your friend is in your PDA or wallet for safe keeping. Even if you do it in front of him, he will be flattered that he matters that much to you. Before this, he probably believed that you were too busy to be such an amazing listener, let alone to document what he says!

Now, you get to be creative. It's fun to think about what material objects might be related to what's important to him. You can brainstorm while you're driving, standing in line, or waiting for that next webpage to download.

Here's an example:
Your friend is a Contractor and she talks about things like being the best at her trade, her competition, and her employees. *Possible gifts:* tools, books or magazine subscriptions on new building technology or codes, a level,

contractor software, a fancy graphed notepad set, an aluminum clipboard with a built-in storage box for pens and forms, or a new hardhat.

Here's a more complex example:
Your friend is an Administrative Assistant and he talks about things like his frustrations, going out and getting drunk, his new invention, broken copiers, stupid bosses, and quitting after he wins the lottery.

Possible gifts: the #1 résumé or business plan writing software, a book on protecting your intellectual property, tuition for a class on communication, a gift certificate for a therapeutic massage, a mini-vacation type experience or weekend getaway, a bottle of wine, a journal, or an offer to pass his résumé around Human Resources at yours or a friend's company.

There are no limits to your imagination and focus. Take the obvious and brainstorm on related possibilities, giving yourself total permission to cut loose and be free. Be a genius! Doodle while you explore the unexpected and let each idea connect you to three more. After you have thought of at least 20 possibilities, you can look at what inspires you.

It's your gift to him, so it should inspire you as well. As long as you give yourself enough time, there is nothing to stop you from finding the gift that touches both you and your friend.

Just a reminder: Unless a woman is a carpenter, craftsperson, or has specifically communicated that she wants an appliance like a new dishwasher or a juicer, avoid buying her things that plug in. Usually, this doesn't work in your favor, but tune in to her to make sure.

WE ARE THE CHAMPIONS

All families deal with different kinds of challenges. My family was no exception. When I was about to leave for college and thus begin the emptying of the nest phase, my four siblings and I decided we wanted to give our mother and father something special for Christmas. It had to be something that would bring them peace about the many difficult decisions they had had to make over the years and show how they'd done a great job of raising us.

We found a professional photographer in town, saved our money, and had a formal portrait of us taken that would be ready by Christmas.

Since we were already dressed up in our beiges and light blues, we took pictures in front of our home in Hinsdale, Illinois. It was nearly impossible to get us all in one place at one time, so we took advantage of the moment. As you know, organizing teens is like herding cats. We were always screwing around, and the photos certainly showed how much fun we were having. In the photos, we look like we're happy, well-adjusted, goofy teenagers.

Because my mother had carried the majority of the responsibilities in raising us, I felt like I wanted to do something extra special for her. I used the photographs of us in front of the house to create a photo album from scratch. I combined brass brads to bind together a tan 5x7 framing matte for the cover, black colored paper for the pages, and on the matte used architectural lettering, to rub on the words, "WE ARE THE CHAMPIONS" (taken from a song by Queen – our family theme song) above the best picture.

When Christmas came around, our parents were very happy and surprised by the portraits. My mom was really touched by the effort it took to make it happen and without her ever knowing! She still has the portrait and the album to this day. And, although our father passed away over ten years ago, our step-mom still has our portrait up at their home.

CREATIVE LIST

Stimulate yourself into creative thinking using thought provoking queries about your friend that will lead you to lots of possibilities. Soon you'll have a great list of ideas!

To make the list ask yourself the following questions:

- If I were him, I'd probably like to feel:

- If I were him, I'd probably like to go to:

- If I were him, I'd probably like to have or use:

Consider your friend's desires. There are things you may think he should want or have, things that would be "good for him," but that's not really considering who he is right now. In truth, he is exactly as he wants to be, without changing a thing. If he doesn't ever have time to read, books are probably only useful as door stops. But if he does like stories, you can get him books on CD to make his drives more fun.

As you tune into his world and what it's like to be him, the easier gift giving becomes. Being present with others will come naturally, without thinking about it. Hearing what's really being said automatically connects you with what he would enjoy, and what would bring him pleasure.

It becomes effortless and you begin to feel like the Master of Gift Giving that you already are deep inside. (Remember, intention is everything!)

Sometimes, even you will wonder how you picked such an awesome gift. More importantly, he will look at you with amazement and gratitude. No need to say a word – just smile that charming, mysterious smile of yours!

the Art of
Making Your Gift

IF YOU WANT YOUR GIFT TO BE TRULY CHERISHED, MAKE IT YOURSELF!

There are those who believe that the best gift is one that's personally made by you. Think about all the things you made as a kid, all the pictures you painted, all the popsicle stick cabins you glued, all the footprints and handprints stuck here and there. You know that your parents hung onto them way past their expiration dates – if they don't still have them today!

Five years ago, my boyfriend made a Valentine's Day card for me which I still have. Of course, I still have all the cards he gave me over the past eleven years, but this one will never be stored somewhere, let alone thrown away. It had humor in it, (my worst photograph ever on the front,) words of unconditional love, (my second worst photograph ever inside,) and a lot of time and energy put into the computer graphics and wording. It made me laugh and horrified me at the same time, but he made it and that meant more than any of the expensive cards he's given me over the years.

Making something isn't about saving money, although it is a nice benefit. It's about the time and energy, thought, heart, and soul that you give thinking about this person. It's love incarnate. There is now an object in the universe that didn't exist before, that only exists as an expression of your thoughts and feelings for another.

She inspired you to choose to not do anything else with your thoughts and time, except think of her and how much she would enjoy your gift. While you're making it, you're thinking about; how she will know how much you feel about her, what her reaction might be, her happiness and excitement at receiving it, how she is going to cherish it forever and ever and probably be buried with it. A bought gift just does not have that kind of intense energy, no matter what it is.

It doesn't have to be the only gift you give. It doesn't have to take a lot of time to make. It doesn't even have to be artistic or beautiful.

It just has to be made by you.

If you like to work with wood, you can get wonderful plaques, boxes, and interesting sculptural pieces at craft stores that you can simply paint with acrylic paints. Sponge brushes make it easy and fast.

If you like to sew, bead, arrange flowers, or sculpt, the same goes for you – go to any craft store and you'll get an abundance of ideas.

It doesn't matter what it is, if it's from your heart, it will be cherished. If you're listening to your loved one, you'll think of lots of things that she could use or would love to look at.

Make It Yourself Ideas

She loves landscapes: paint an abstract landscape on canvas with acrylic paint. Choose colors that go with the room it might hang in. Copy a simple abstract from an art or interior design magazine.

He has lots of watches or spare change: buy an unfinished wooden box and paint or stain it, then cover it with Mod Podge®.

She likes to do crafts: build her an organizer that keeps all the little crafty knick knacks separate and easy to find.

He loves sports: sew a canvas duffel or tote bag to carry all his equipment from his house to the field. Paint a wooden box for the all the TV remotes. Stick with the colors of his favorite team.

She travels a lot: make elegant shoe bags to keep her clothes clean from dirty shoes.

Not so crafty? Hire a professional photographer to take a sexy portrait of you, then matte and frame it yourself.

It doesn't matter what you make, it really is the thought that counts. If you put your heart into whatever you make, you will get MEGAPOINTS for trying.

the Art of
Event Coordinating

SURPRISE EVENTS!

Once you know your friend's hopes, dreams and aspirations, you'll also know what kind of event or experience would surprise and delight him. You can easily find out people's contact information through best friends, relatives, or colleagues. If people know you're going to arrange something wonderful for him, you'll find more support and ideas than you could imagine. Everyone loves to play a part in giving someone a special, thoughtful gift, especially if it's an organized event, concert, club night, orchestrated dinner, or surprise party!

Organize his close friends and family members to celebrate getting together for bowling, miniature golf, dinner at a casual or fancy restaurant, pizza delivery, coffee and dessert, a movie, a museum, art gallery, or amusement park trip.

SUPER HIP BOWLING

My boyfriend worked at a very upscale Hollywood entertainment company for over six years, and everyone who worked there was very cool. One year, I invited all our friends, including his cool colleagues, for a surprise birthday bowling party at Jerry's Famous Deli, which has a bowling alley in the back. We had balloons, hats, and noisemakers – the whole shebang. It was embarrassing.

This was his first surprise birthday party. He was sort of in shock, smiling and laughing the whole night. We have pictures of him bowling with balloons tied all over his body, including his head! Everyone had fantastic fun, especially the cool colleagues! They got to cut loose and just be themselves. Things like bowling and miniature golf are great for connecting people in a pressure free, casual, fun way.

My boyfriend became very present to how much he was loved and appreciated, and by so many people. This may have also been another first. He never expected his co-workers would come to such a potentially "dorky" party. You never know how little it takes to shift the way someone sees the world, and even more importantly, how they feel about themselves.

You could invite his friends and family to a play, musical, favorite film, art show, fair, or festival. Make sure to coordinate the purchase of the tickets in time to get the seats you want.

Coordinate a short flight or train ride to a local tourist spot or entertaining city. You could ask everyone to get all dressed up and have dinner at a nice hotel. You'll almost feel like you're on vacation for a few hours. You're creating memorable and special moments that will never be forgotten. Get three disposable cameras, pass them around for everyone to shoot whatever they want, and then collect them at the end of the event for really fun photos!

Super cheesy experiences can be so freeing – they get people to break out of their shells and be more spontaneous, silly, and expressive!

Take your friend on a surprise budgeted shopping spree, either with gift certificates or better – fun, free-wheeling cash. Make sure to keep the specifics clearly communicated, so it remains a great experience for you, too!

If it's something really special like a 50th Wedding Anniversary and you have the budget, how about taking the whole family to Aspen for skiing, snowboarding, shopping, and sleigh rides, or Santa Fe for art galleries, great restaurants, Navajo jewelry, and pueblo dances? These gorgeous places have something for everyone.

How about a trip to a country that he's always talked about visiting?

My mother has always loved and read about Africa. Someday, I would love to take her there. How will you know where that sacred place might be? Is his whole house decorated in Scottish plaids? Does he play the didjeradoo, have a kangaroo salt-and-pepper shaker collection, and keeps asking, "How 'bout anotha shrimp on the baarbie?" There are always signs. You don't have to be a brain surgeon to figure it out.

And you can creatively coordinate events that aren't surprises. They don't have to be a big secret. Everyone can be in on the preparations.

THE GRAND CANYON

For Christmas a few years ago, my mother, sister, and I organized a family gathering in Flagstaff, Arizona and the Grand Canyon, which included my mother, my step-mother, two sisters, two brothers, one brother-in-law, one niece, one boyfriend and his parents. Our families aren't wealthy and we weren't sure how everyone would get along, but we kept within a budget and this holiday brought out the best in everyone. Everyone knew this Christmas was special and something that would probably not happen very often.

We stayed at an extraordinarily Christmas-y hotel called Little America. My boyfriend's mother made the most amazing Norwegian foods bringing everything, including wonderful room decorations, for a delicious and cheerful Christmas!

One of my brothers was working in Sri Lanka over Christmas, so he emailed a digital video of his Christmas morning, which made us all feel closer to him, and that made Christmas complete. When even one of us isn't there, it feels like half the family is missing.

Most of us had never been to the Grand Canyon before. It was truly awe-inspiring and fun. We all had a chance to spend quality time with our three year old niece. It was an experience beyond anyone's expectations – a cherished holiday never to be forgotten. It took a lot of work and time to arrange, but the memories will last a lifetime.

Every ounce of love you put into these experiences multiply that love for everyone else a thousand fold. Never underestimate the power of your intentions to make people happy. In the process of acting on your impulses to give joy to others, you'll get to experience a rare peace and contentment within. Acknowledge and appreciate yourself for being that most amazing of humans, a giver.

There's a perspective out there that makes givers think there's something wrong with them. Thinking about others all the time – how co-dependent! How doormat! Not if you're giving to yourself first, and then sharing your overflow. Then there's an endless supply. Then you're just a pure, generous giver – with no ulterior motives.

Just watch how much flows back to you now!

the Art of
Creative Projects

You will hear your friend speak about the people who matter to her/him. This list of people will give you BIG CLUES to the companions with whom she chooses to go to dinner, a show, or on a trip. For obvious reasons, it's very important to write these names down ASAP. (We barely remember the names of people we just met!)

A GREAT GIFT FROM EVERYONE TO GIVE AT THE PARTY

Getting everyone to participate makes it so much more meaningful. You can ask some of her/his friends and colleagues to help create a scrapbook of writings and photographs. Here's a sample letter for inviting people to make this an extremely special gift for your friend:

"Dear Friends of (your friend's name,)

Since (friend) is having a birthday coming up, I thought it would mean a lot to (her/him) to have letters, poems, and photos from people who've been important to (her/him) over the years. I'd like (friend) to know they've made a positive impact on many lives, and you come to mind in that regard, because I know you've made a big impact on (her/him.)

If you want to send something but can't think of anything, here are a few ideas: a paragraph of a special memory of a time spent with (friend), what characteristics you like about (her/him,) or something (she/he's) said or did that you still remember (a positive memory, of course), an old photo with a brief story, a long note on stationery, a poem, song, or matchbook, relating to your memories or thoughts about (friend) as (she/he) approaches (her/his) __th birthday. Another option is to contribute a fun, outrageous, or sentimental birthday card with a short personal note inside. If I have any photos that fit with what you send, I'll add them.

(We're/I'm) going to be giving it to (friend) on (her/his) birthday on (date.) Please try to get your stuff to me by (date) – (make it at least a week before the needed date) in order to give me time to put it all together. You can send it to: (name and address.) (Make sure this address is not where your friend will see it and ruin the surprise!)

Thank you for participating in making this a great birthday for (friend)!

All good things,

(YOUR NAME)

the Art of
Staying Within Budget
and On Time

Know Your Budget
Before You Start

If you know how much you want to spend up front, you won't go overboard or be swayed by new ideas, amazing products, or well-intended helpers. Stay focused and clear, and stay within your budget. This ensures that you will have a good experience and continue to enjoy giving unique gifts long into the future.

Allow 20% of Your Budget
for Gift-wrap, Shipping,
and The Card

You can spend about 80% of your budget on the gift itself, but remember that there's more. The gift-wrap, shipping, if necessary, and most importantly, The Card!

Start Two Weeks Ahead of the Event

Preparation! Preparation! Preparation!

Because we're all very busy these days, it's important to schedule time in advance to shop, perhaps online or at your favorite mall, free of distractions and pressures. The more relaxed you are about finding the perfect way to acknowledge and appreciate your friend, the more creative and successful your results.

Your goal should be to complete preparations at least one week ahead of the date. Give yourself plenty of time and space – at least a week to work on the plan, whether it's shopping, card writing, wrapping, organizing, making a scrapbook, or planning a trip.

the Art of Presentation

THE MOST IMPORTANT ITEM: THE CARD!

The Card is important because it is your chance to literally acknowledge and appreciate your friend in permanent, long-lasting, concrete WORDS! Here you get to put into your own words proof that you really do hear, understand, see, and care about her. If you have a hard time putting your feelings into clear words, ask for help. There are always people around who are good writers and can help you articulate those things. Start by giving them a draft of what you want to say – even if it's in pictographs!

Often, what kind of Card, and what you say in The Card written by hand, matters more to your friend than the gift – as it should. You could just sign your name, but that isn't really being a Master Gift Giver. Take a minute to say what you appreciate about her. Again, remember to make it about her, not you.

It means more when it comes from your heart than any material object you could possibly purchase. If all you do is find a poem from a book or on the internet and copy it by hand into The Card (giving credit to the poetess/poet, of course,) you will find it will have a powerful impact on your friend. It will probably touch her much more than she expresses at the time, and definitely more than your gift will. Her feelings of being inspired or touched by your Card will last a lot longer than your gift as well.

I know...then why get her a gift at all?

The Gift says:
I listen to you and get what matters to you. This is a token of my caring about you.

The Card says:
This is what I appreciate about you and this is specifically how I feel about you.

Wrapping It Up!

The Gift Wrap you can go wild on and have someone at Bloomingdale's or the Party Store wrap for you. The fancier the paper, gift bags, ribbons, and bows – the better. It makes her feel special and valued by you, unless you're just having it done so that you don't have to deal with it.

If it's a gift from your five year old, wrap it in pages from your child's coloring book or art from school. You probably have boxes of it that you just can't throw away.

If you're 15-100 years old, you could be creative and tie the wrapping style in with the gift or to her hobbies or career. If it's a Chinese Feng Shui gift like crystals or small chimes, try wrapping it in a Chinese take out carton with red ribbons and chopsticks as decoration. If it's sports themed such as golf balls, get wrapping paper with a golf theme and tape golf tees at the base of the bow or ribbons. If the person is a music lover, wrap it in sheet music from a flea market or music store. For a real estate broker, wrap it in pictures of homes or buildings torn from magazines and newspapers. For an electrician, use an extension cord as ribbon. There are endless ways to tie it in.

Russian Doll Wrapping

For tickets to a show or a trip, you could put them in an envelope and then do what my boyfriend's mom does. Put the envelope in a slightly bigger box, and then wrap it in a larger package. Then put that wrapped package into an even larger package or box and wrap that. It's along the lines of the Russian dolls – six to twelve small dolls within a gradually larger doll – but you're doing it with different kinds of containers.

One of the containers could be a teddy bear backpack or something cute like that. This is great for those people who always guess what their gift is before they even open it! It completely throws them off the scent. Some of the boxes or bags could be gifts in and of themselves. This is great for kids and adults. It just adds fun, prolongs attention on the receiver and stretches out the surprise!

You might want to avoid the diamond ring inside dessert trick! Practice foresight and keep possibilities for disaster out of the picture.

How you present the gift to your friend is important, too. Your actions speak louder than words. There's a huge difference between someone tossing a gift to you, or to having it presented grandly, unexpectedly and fabulously. Making your presentation unique and momentous will make her feel happy, surprised, and special.

"How great I must be to receive such a cherished present!"

And isn't that your goal?

Although there are the rare few who hate surprises, a real surprise totally unexpected and presented with authentic caring and the wish to please, delights everyone!

And what a reward for all your listening, caring, coordinating, and energy!

the Art of Knowing Where to Look

THE INTERNET

If you have a computer, searching online first really helps you be creative and saves a lot of time and gas. But be focused! The internet is very distracting, as well!

GOOGLE IT!

www.google.com is a great website for searches, but any browser will do.

DIRECTIONS

These two sites are great for directions:
www.mapquest.com
www.maps.google.com

For scrapbooks and journals, first get your friend's best friend's number or email address to surreptitiously get a "friends and family" contact list. E-mailing takes the least amount of effort in initially coordinating people, but don't rely on e-mail for finalizing important details and logistics. E-mail is not communication. Use the phone. It will be well worth it, and will take less time than you think.

Scrapbooks and journals can be obtained from: Barnes and Noble, Amazon, Borders, Aaron Brothers, Papyrus, Target, or Michael's Craft Stores.

Ticketmaster.com is a great source for show and concert tickets. Expedia.com, travelocity.com, biddingfortravel.com, and priceline.com are great for discount travel fares, trip information and other links.

If you don't have access to a computer, just browse some catalogs or go to your favorite shops or malls. This should be fun for you, above all, or it will most likely rarely happen again. There are millions of great small shops and stores that carry unique hard to find things, and some of them are right in your neighborhood!

The following website and product suggestions are a few of my favorites. Many sites have catalogs online which saves trees! Each website you go to will lead you to other similar products and new ideas. You will know when you've found the perfect gift by the deep breath you take when you find it, that says what you want to say, meets your budget, and can be delivered in plenty of time to keep you from panicking at the last minute.

Leaving yourself at least a week for delays, also gives you the most cost effective shipping choices. Almost everything you order online that you need rushed, increases the cost exponentially.

GREAT GIFTS FOR WOMEN

Pampering Her	www.spafinder.com
Rich Scent Candles	www.blushcandles.com
Cell Bling Ring Kit	www.myblingring.com
Sexy Things	wholisticwisdom.com
Clothing	www.nordstrom.com
Book: Office Spa	www.amazon.com
Inspirational	www.hayhouse.com
Jewelry	www.katyadesigns.com
Travel	women-traveling.com
Jewelry/Furniture	www.overstock.com
Wealthy Woman	www.richwoman.com
Body Image	www.elemental-films.com
Aromatherapy	www.funlittlethings.com
Special Teas	www.adagio.com
Jewelry Boxes	www.beautyrose.com
Great Chocolate	neuhauschocolateshop.com
Laptop Bags	www.penelopebags.com
Great Luggage	www.mckleinusa.com
Plants/Flowers	www.redenvelope.com
iRobot Vacuum	www.hsn.com
Evian Brumisateur	www.satinbox.com

 # GREAT GIFTS FOR TEEN GIRLS

Fly Pen Computer	www.toysrus.com
iPod® Necklace	www.bloomingdales.com
Fashion	www.karmaloop.com
Wall Décor	www.urbanoutfitters.com
Homework Holder	www.pbteen.com
Book: Generation T	www.bn.com
Posters	www.allposters.com
Vegetables Rock!	www.borders.com
Self-Esteem Doc	www.elemental-films.com
Adopt-A-Pet	www.petfinder.com

GREAT GIFTS FOR MEN

Tech Toys	www.compusa.com
Computers	www.frys.com
TV/DVD's	www.bestbuy.com
QC3 Headphones	www.bose.com
Aeron Chairs	www.sit4less.com
Luxury Pens	www.cross.com
Fine Art	www.arttracks.com
Netflix	www.netflix.com
Relationship Toys	fromaphrodite.com
The StressEraser	www.stresseraser.com
Sports Guy	www.sportchalet.com
Party Table	www.bingbongtables.com
Style Guy	www.gievesandhawkes.com
Bluetooth Eyewear	www.sharperimage.com
Gadgets	www.engadget.com
Tools	www.lowes.com
Model Trains	www.etrainshop.com
Electronics	www.tomshardware.com
Automotive	www.cartalk.com
BBQ Branding Iron	www.personalcreations.com

 ## GREAT GIFTS FOR TEEN GUYS

Video Gamer	www.gamespy.com
Board Games	www.kidsworld.com
Ant Gel Habitat	www.dsc.discovery.com
Lego Kits	www.target.com
Model Kits	www.megahobby.com
Rich Dad for Teens	www.amazon.com
iPod®	www.apple.com
Pen Scanner	www.photoalley.com
Mod Bistro Scooter	www.shop.com
Cashflow 101	www.richdad.com

GREAT GIFTS FOR CHILDREN

Monograms	www.gardenlane.com
Prince(ss) Tricycle	www.laylagrayce.com
Learning Laptops	www.etoys.com
Storybook Publisher	www.dsc.discovery.com
Aqua Doodle	www.target.com
Thomas the Train	www.allaboardtoys.com
Clothing	www.childrensplace.com
Aquariums	www.etoys.com
Development	www.leapfrog.com
Inflatable Giraffe	www.hammacher.com
Brain Age	www.brainage.com
Family Fun Game	www.cranium.com
Standing Easel	www.oliebollen.com
Organizers	www.ikea.com
Sew Fun Kit	www.dsc.discovery.com
Kid-Tough Camera	www.fisherprice.com
Dora The Explorer	www.nextag.com
Baby Minds	www.babyeinstein.com
Baby Bedding	dreamsoftbedware.com
Baby Clothes	www.malinas.com

 ## GREAT GIFTS FOR COLLEAGUES

Business 2.0 Mag	www.business20.com
Dinosaur Plant	scientificsonline.com
Tiki Tissue Cover	www.target.com
Goofy Office Toys	www.perpetualkid.com
Auto-Putt	www.golfworks.com
NAP Travel Kit	www.brookstone.com
Global Alarm Clock	www.frontgate.com
Women of Style	www.anthropologie.com
Self Stirring Mug	www.hammacher.com
Office Fish Tank	www.target.com

GREAT GIFTS FOR HEALTH, WEALTH & THE GREAT OUTDOORS

Organic Clothing	katequinnorganics.com
Healthy Products	www.shopnatural.com
Animal Friendly	www.peta.com
Body Care	www.thebodyshop.com
Baseball Gloves	www.carpentertrade.com
Feng Shui	uniquefengshuishop.com
Non-Leather Shoes	www.mooshoes.com
Eco Wear	www.ecolution.com
Vegan Wear	www.veganstore.com
Peterson Guides	www.petersononline.com
Exercise Gear	www.rei.com
Equipment	www.costco.com
Renewable Energy	www.ecomall.com
Millionaire Course	www.marcallen.com
Millionaire Mind	millionairemind.com
Organic Body	www.aubreyorganics.com
Sno Forts & Tubes	www.sportsstuff.com
Messenger Bags	www.tombihn.com
Prius Hybrid Car	www.toyota.com/prius/
Healthy Food	www.wildoats.com

 # GREAT WEDDING GIFTS

Sur La Table	www.surlatable.com
Genealogy Tree	www.redenvelope.com
Dinner Cruises	www.gifts.com
Napa Valley Trip	www.aubergedusoleil.com
Carafe	www.crateandbarrel.com
Allergy Free	www.livingincomfort.com
Personal Doormats	smithandhawken.com
Power of Now CD	www.eckharttolle.com
Crystal Doves	www.eluxury.com

GREAT PET GIFTS

Dog Toys	naturalpetmarket.com
Sushi Dog Toys	www.perpetualkid.com
Natural Treats	www.barkaroobakery.com
Designer Pet Beds	www.barkingbaby.com
Ra-Cat-A-Sac	www.drsfostersmith.com
Styled Pet Carriers	www.chimpfeet.com
Elevated Feeders	www.jefferspet.com
Dog Spa Basket	www.yourdogwilldigit.com
Pet Portraits	yazhipetportraits.com
Dog Lips Chew Toy	www.orvis.com
Drinkwell Fountain	thecatconnection.com
Pill Pockets	www.drsfostersmith.com
CatTreat Cookbook	www.overstock.com
Missing Link	www.petvetdirect.com

GREAT WEBSITES

Great Gift Ideas	www.gifts.com
	www.target.com
Great Deals	www.ebay.com
Books	www.amazon.com
DVD's	www.bn.com
CD's	www.borders.com
Fine Living TV	www.fineliving.com
Travel Deal Guide	www.biddingfortravel.com
Travel Deals	www.priceline.com
Travel Channel	www.travelchannel.com
I Want That!	marketplace.hgtv.com
Top Spas	www.concierge.com
Spiritual Retreats	www.findhorn.org
Abiquiu Retreat	www.ghostranch.org

GREAT GIFTS FROM CHILDREN

To make holiday shopping as easy as possible for you and your kids, here are few suggestions. Have them make a list of who they're shopping for. Next to the names, ask them to write down how much they want to spend on each person. To teach them about budgeting, give them a dollar amount that they can spend. (For the older kids ready to learn about hidden costs, make sure they include the cost of The Card and possible shipping.)

Give your children catalogs, markers and plenty of time to circle their choices. Before heading out, give them a wallet or zip lock bag with their list and budget in cash. When you get to the stores, give them a time limit on each store.

If the store doesn't have it in stock, some gifts may be ordered online, so deduct that amount from their cash budget with them at the computer, so they can see that it costs money ordering online, too.

After you get home (and take a breather!) have them fill out The Card and wrap the gift, to keep the momentum up and the spirit of giving high. It will come across in their Cards!

the Art of Gracious Giving

In order to give a gift graciously, you'll have to go out and get some Humility. That, I'm afraid, I don't know where you can get. (I barely have any.) It has to do with putting your thoughts that are "all about you" on the back burner, while someone else shines. It means avoiding the temptation to tell him all you went through to make it happen. Save that story for later, and only if asked. It takes a lot of will power, especially if you're used to being the center of attention, or at least the center of Your World. It's a generous feeling to want someone else to "own" the day or night.

A huge part of your gift is your willingness to be invisible for a few short hours, while the person you care about stands in the limelight, with all the praise and glory going to him, fulfilling him, and making him glad he was born.

If you have a true desire to please your friend, it comes through. You can watch him enjoying himself and your gift, knowing that he will truly know all that you did to make this perfect. For a few hours, I know you can resist telling all your stories about "me," "my process," and "what I did for you." Keep the conversation on him to complete the giving process. And if and when you do speak, remember to make it acknowledgements and appreciation for him. This is his Moment of Glory, not yours, no matter how much you did.

the Art of
Gracious Receiving

Just as important as knowing how to give, is knowing how to receive – how to graciously receive. It starts with feeling that you deserve to receive.

Not a sense of entitlement, as much as a feeling of being a good person, being a deserving person, and someone for whom people would wish blessings and good things. Practice feeling like that person.

Maybe you don't want to receive, because you don't feel you deserve anything good coming to you. Maybe you only want to receive a certain quality of things, and you don't value what's being given to you.

If you want the person who loves you to feel powerful and valuable, empower her by receiving her gifts graciously.

Allow her to express her wish to make you happy, which actually reinforces her sense of being capable, competent, and worthy. You're giving them a gift by realizing how much you matter to them – communicating that what they have to give is appreciated and important to you.

When someone gives you a gift, be humbly grateful and acknowledge their desire to make you happy and the great impact they have in your life.

the Art of
Giving to Yourself

Hey! What about you? You, the Master Gift Giver, have deep needs yourself, which may or may not be getting acknowledged or met. You're the only one who can know and fulfill these needs.

Discover what they are and go through this gift giving process with you as the recipient first. As goofy as it sounds, get over it, and create the time to give yourself memorable experiences and gifts. You could even take pictures that will remind you of these precious self-honoring moments.

GIVING MYSELF THE
GIFT OF GOOD HEALTH

I wanted to give myself a healthier body and greater energy, so I joined a health club with one of my best friends. I made sure that I wouldn't quit by being accountable to her for going three times a week. After every ten workouts we do together, we give ourselves a luxurious reward – we go to a hot springs spa for a day of total relaxation!

We're both people who are very into our work and goals, so as luscious as it sounds, getting to the spa is a real challenge. It takes extreme deliberation to get us to focus on our bodies – even though it feels great once we're there!

Life and work always seem to take precedence. It's been ten months, and we definitely aren't perfect at it, but we're still committed and making it happen.

Surrounding myself with supportive, unconditional friends who make sure I'm self-nourishing is the only way that works for me. Maybe someday, it will be such a deeply ingrained habit that I won't need anyone to remind me to be good to myself!

On Being More Selfish

You can't give what you don't have. We, as caring individuals, can never be poor, sick, or miserable enough to make someone else wealthy, healthy, or happy. Life doesn't work like that. Every person is selfish, or the human species would not have survived this long.

You can only give to others to the degree that you have already given to yourself. I believe that it's healthy to be selfish in order to feel fulfilled and content. Only then do we actually have the capability to give generously and unconditionally, no longer giving to get or demanding return on our investment. Our abundance then overflows freely and naturally. When we give unconditionally, we have the power to be a great society where all people are able to flourish and contribute.

To be respectful and value ourselves, it takes courage to create and maintain healthy boundaries with the people who surround us. It takes courage to consistently choose to truly nourish ourselves, regardless of what others think. Each of us is a unique being. It takes lots of searching to learn what nourishes us, but when we're overflowing from within, there's no end to what we can give.

WHAT DO I WANT?

That's the most important question you can ask for your life. Take the time to really get clear about what you want for yourself. Each person is completely different from everyone else. Sometimes it's hard to separate what you want from what other people want you to want. Look at who you really are, and what makes you happy in all the areas of your life; physical, emotional, mental, spiritual, psychological, home, friends, family, career, creativity, travel, transportation, and recreation.

There are many people these days who want the time and space to just be and express themselves freely. You may want a vacation from life. You don't have to go to Hawaii or Tuscany to gift yourself the time and space to do and be whatever you want. You could give yourself the gift of spending a half-hour every day just sitting in your room doing nothing. (You probably spend way more than that in a day just watching TV commercials!) You could give yourself permission to take time on your way home from work each day to go to your favorite café, get a cup of tea or coffee, and read your favorite magazine or a few pages from a good book. There are things you imagine that "other" lucky people get to do that you don't dream of allowing yourself to do. Try imagining what you would do if you were a billionaire and could do anything you want. What would you do? How would you be generous with yourself?

Be that billionaire now in your treatment of yourself. There's nothing stopping you from using your imagination. Use the luxury of time and space to choose to do and be what makes you happy. In the history of humanity, we have never had more freedom, abundance, and awareness to choose powerfully how we live our lives on a daily basis.

Maybe it is time to take a trip to Italy or New Zealand to honor yourself and your dreams. Share your desires with your best friend and ask him to support you in making that your reality. There's less of a chance that you'll chicken out or put yourself on the back burner for some other "priority."

If you feel like you need a trip to Home Depot or Victoria's Secret with an unlimited time constraint, choose a date, put it on your calendar, set aside the time, and be aware that this is YOU appreciating YOU, and showing it with a GIFT. Get your self-appreciation out of your head and into physical action.

If you need a new bicycle, Prius, Cadillac, trip to Disney World or to China, let yourself know that you are worthy of your own appreciation and of pleasuring yourself.

Wrap the tickets in a card with a note of acknowledgement to yourself. (I know, you'll feel stupid, just do it anyway and tell me how it felt afterwards. And stop worrying about what others think of you! If you haven't noticed, they're mostly thinking about themselves anyway. Who cares? It's YOUR LIFE! This is it!)

Honor yourself with the gift, and then decide when you're going to give it to yourself. Make this an occasion of self-love and appreciation. This is a great way to really feel acknowledged. The only way to ever feel these loving acknowledgements is to feel them about yourself. After that, others can reinforce or reflect them, but they can only start with you.

the Art of
Remembering

Visual reminders work the best for me. If I don't have it written somewhere, odds are, I won't be taking any action on it for a long time. When something is important, tell yourself that it's important enough to write down and place where you can manage the information easily.

Always find the system that works for you. If you rebel against your own systems, it just makes your life harder. It's up to you.

To remember what you've learned here, you may want to make a copy of this little reminder and put it in your wallet or purse!

THE ART OF GIFT GIVING

1. Your BIG CLUE: Her Excited Emotions!
2. Who is this person? What is important to him?
3. Your Listening & Forgiving are the
   Greatest Gifts you can give Everyday!
4. Give from your overflow
5. Write down every creative idea you get!
6. Surprise Events? Get best friend's cell # or email
7. Being Generous - No stories on "me, myself, I"
8. Acknowledge & Appreciate yourself & others often

the Art of Wholeness

Now that you see people in a new light, acknowledge yourself for the courage it takes to be your greatest self. To be present with another is to love what is right here and now exactly as it is, without trying to change anything, without manipulation, without fixing or improving.

And accepting the way things are just as they are is what wholeness feels like. Wholeness within yourself.

Being completely comfortable with everything that is here in your life right now gives you the ability to flow true gifts to yourself and to others, from a real place – you.

the Art of
Forgiving

THE TWO GREATEST GIFTS YOU CAN EVER GIVE ARE: LISTENING & FORGIVING

Life is full of surprises, weirdness, great experiences, clarity, love, communication, lines crossed, misunderstandings, kindness, creativity, lessons, realizations, beliefs, egos run amuck, generosity, sanity, insanity, and emotional baggage.

It's a rich and wondrous gift we've been given to experience so much in just a few short years. We might live 80 – 100 years in relation to the 4.5 billion year old Earth. We have some time here to do some stuff, try to make a difference, and then we go. The population is increasing and there's much more human interaction and communication than ever before.

People come from so many different cultures, beliefs, perspectives, educations, religions, childhood experiences, and aspirations. We all have excellent reasons for being the way we are at any given moment. And we all keep changing!

Strangely enough, most of us would prefer it if everyone else were just a little more… something else. We don't know what exactly, but we definitely know when they're not being it. Maybe we're so critical of ourselves that it's all we can do *not* to lash out, to distract us from seeing what we don't approve of in ourselves.

But what does making them wrong give us, really?

Nothing. It leaves us empty and sad when we are so very right and everyone else is so very wrong. At what cost are we right? At what cost do we protect ourselves from those jerks? What do we gain from creating the thickest wall – the one that no-one ever penetrated again? Is there an award somewhere? Will I get a trophy for being so safe that I'm never hurt again?

We're living in a world where if we don't Master the Art of Forgiveness, starting with forgiving ourselves, we'll definitely lose the war. Not just the war, we'll actually lose everything, including our lovely hostess, the Earth – our extraordinary, gorgeous, bountiful Earth.

There are so many things I'd like to be forgiven for. So many friends I've hurt over the years, always unintentionally, but I'm sure it didn't feel like that to them.

And I've been hurt plenty. I've got excellent reasons not to forgive. I blamed my parents for my psychological limitations until I was in my forties. I believed they made poor choices that permanently damaged my self-esteem, and deep down I was all about proving me right and them wrong by sub-consciously sacrificing my success. That's how far the ego will go to be right, mine anyway.

This is insanity. This polarized win-lose thinking is insanity and we can either stay on the ride, or consciously choose to get off every minute of every day. That's about what it takes to constantly let it all go: the right, wrong, good, evil, win, lose, first, last, looking good, competing to validate oneself, fighting to not; lose any ground, lose face, lose respect, lose authority, lose one-upmanship, and lose (non-existent) power.

The simplest way to gain sanity and become a Master Gift Giver is to forgive – forgive everything forever. Forgive everyone and yourself everything forever. Seriously.

Here's what I have on my mirror and I say it everyday as many times as I can:

I forgive everyone and myself everything, forever.

This gift is like a boomerang. You give it all away, and you keep getting more back. (Okay, a boomerang doesn't give you more back, but you get the picture.)

What you'll notice is that you feel free. Every time you think it, you'll feel like you just received the most amazing gift ever – freedom and a sense of lightness. Isn't that why you go on vacation – to feel those feelings? All the chains of blame dissolve. It brings you into the present moment with every possibility open to you.

With all the blame, compulsive proving, rationalizing and wrong-making gone, it feels like you're floating. The noises stop. It's quiet and you feel a sense of peace.

I forgive everyone and myself everything, forever.

Can you imagine if you knew someone who listened to you without taking their eyes off you, hanging onto every word, whether or not they agreed with you, truly getting who you are and what you're trying to communicate? Can you imagine someone who you had lots of ups and downs with and saw things so diametrically different than you do, but forgave you everything? What would it be like to be in the presence of someone who forgave themselves everything? Who forgave you everything, forever?

Imagine that you are that person who truly listens and truly forgives everyone and themselves everything, forever.

Gifts and Cards are lovely symbols and reminders of kindness, compassion and generosity of spirit and power – your Spirit and your Power on this planet.

But to give the gifts that keep on giving, give your listening and your forgiveness, forever.

You will be known for it as one of the most generous of people, a source of true Power and impact, the greatest of Gift Givers.

You are a Master Gift Giver!

Epilogue

When you are GIVING, you are BEING:

generous
present
accepting
forgiving
understanding
compassionate
patient
humble
observant
creative
whole
inspired
&
inspiring!

Thank you for being an inspiration to me. The fact that
you have the desire to be a Master Gift Giver, is a miracle.
It shows who you are in the world. It shows how many
people you must have touched already. It shows that –
You Make a Difference!
Thank you for being who you are!

To order more copies of

the Art of
GIFT GIVING™

Go to
Lulu Publishing
www.lulu.com

Private Gift Giving Consultations
are available with Shereen Elise Noon

(310) 497-0597
snoon@elemental-films.com

3015846